GodSpeaks™

Devotional

Honor Books
Tulsa, Oklahoma

GodSpeaks™ Devotional
ISBN 1-56292-857-0
Copyright © 2000 by Honor Books
P.O. Box 55388
Tulsa, Oklahoma 74155

Let's meet at my house Sunday before the game.

C'mon over and bring the kids.

What part of "Thou Shalt Not" didn't you understand?

We need to talk.

Keep using my name in vain, I'll make rush hour longer.

Loved the wedding, invite me to the marriage.

That "Love Thy Neighbor" thing . . . I meant that.

I love you. I love you. I love you.

Will the road you're on get you to my place?

Follow me.

Need directions?

You think it's hot here?

Tell the kids I love them.

Need a marriage counselor? I'm available.

Have you read my #1 best-seller? (There will be a test.)

Do you have any idea where you're going?

"Big Bang Theory"? You've got to be kidding.

My way *is* the highway.

Introduction

God has a lot to say, and He has said it pretty plainly within the framework of the Bible. But, despite the fact that the Bible is one of the best known and most widely read books on the planet, most people really aren't familiar with how its concepts and principles fit into their everyday lives.

If you are one of those people, this book has been designed especially for you. The statements attributed to God are, of course, not His actual words. They are, however, statements that illustrate principles He taught in the Bible. We hope that they will cause you to meditate on God's character, question some of your preconceived notions, and discover for yourself the personal nature of His love and care for you.

We also hope you will be inspired by the devotionals and amused by this unabashed approach. If you have questions or would like to make comments, please feel free to contact us at our Web site: www.GodSpeaks.org

Let's talk.
—GOD

Call to me and I will answer you and tell you great and unsearchable things.

Jeremiah 33:3

The God of the entire universe wants to have a conversation with you! Can you imagine that? It's amazing but true.

Most of us would consider it the opportunity of a lifetime to meet and talk with our favorite movie star, professional athlete, or recording artist. We look up to these people. We are impressed and influenced and inspired by them. But how quickly and how often do we pass up the chance to talk to God, who is more interesting and more important than any person we could ever revere.

The Lord God created it all—including the celebrities we admire so much. He created us specifically to have a relationship with Him. And the only way to have a relationship with anyone is to spend time talking to him or her. What more important relationship could you build? What better way could you spend your time than getting to know God? He has all the answers.

The Master of the universe is waiting. You may not know Him, but He knows you, and He wants to hear from you. There is no risk. You have nothing to lose. Don't wait another second. Close your eyes and open your heart, God wants to talk to you today!

C'mon over and bring the kids.
—GOD

Jesus said, "Let the little children come to me, and do not hinder them, for the kingdom of heaven belongs to such as these."

Matthew 19:14

A partially deaf boy came home from school one day, carrying a note from his teachers. The note suggested that the parents take the boy out of school, claiming that he was "too stupid to learn." The boy's mother read the note and said, "My son Tom isn't stupid. I'll teach him myself." And she did just that.

When Tom died many years later, the people of the United States of America paid tribute to him by turning off the nation's lights for one full minute. You see, this Tom had invented the lightbulb—and motion pictures, the record player, and more than one thousand other items.

No child is beyond learning, and no child is beyond experiencing a close and intimate relationship with God. Over and over, the Bible says that God welcomes children with open arms. Jesus blessed them, held them on His lap, and told His disciples not to hinder them. Children were welcome wherever He went.

Whether you are reaching out to God for the first time or nurturing a long and satisfying relationship with Him, don't hesitate to share what you have found with the children in your life. God will be delighted!

My way *is* the highway.
—GOD

As the heavens are higher than the earth,
so are my ways higher than your ways,
and my thoughts than your thoughts.

Isaiah 55:9

Have you ever tried explaining something to a two-year-old child? Sometimes small children just don't seem to be able to understand what we tell them, especially our answers to that never-ending question: "Why?"

In our "information-rich" world, we have figured out so much. And like a child who can't understand why he or she can't touch the moon or eat candy for every meal, we question God. It is easy to forget that what we know is a tiny drop in the immeasurable ocean of God's knowledge.

In the Bible, God tells us that His ways are much higher than our ways and that we can comprehend only a tiny piece of His master plan. God has promised us that His way is the only way and that if we follow Him, everything will ultimately work out for our good. This doesn't mean that everything that happens is good. It just means that even the most horrific, terrible stories can have happy endings when we place our trust in God.

Open your heart to see God in His primary role—Master Architect of the universe. Then remember that He has chosen to reach past the sun, the moon, and the stars in order to take your hand.

Have you read my #1 best-seller?

(There will be a test.)
—GOD

*Your word is a lamp to my feet
and a light for my path.*

Psalm 119:105

Did you know that the Holy Bible is the best-selling, most-read book in the entire history of the world? It's had a profound impact on Western civilization from its beginning.

Chances are, you have a Bible somewhere in your home, even if it's just gathering dust on the coffee table. You've tried to understand it. You even started out with a great plan to read it from Genesis to Revelation and then got sidetracked in the middle of the section that told who "begat" whom. "It's just too hard!" you groaned.

It's okay. Most people have a hard time with the *King James Version*. It was easy reading for the folks back in the sixteenth century, but the translation is a little difficult for most of us to understand. But don't give up! Did you know there are many modern translations? Not to mention study Bibles, Bibles on tape, study guides, and Bible study groups. No matter what your educational or cultural background, there's something for you.

Once you find a translation that you can understand, God's Word will come alive. It's a book about real people just like you and me, and it contains advice for every situation that you might encounter today. Go ahead. Read it! Find out who God is and how much He loves you.

I love you.
I love you.
I love you.
—GOD

God so loved the world that he gave his one and only Son, that whoever believes in him shall not perish but have eternal life.

John 3:16

What is love? Almost every popular song mentions the concept; most movies and TV shows do as well. But often they aren't talking about real love. The "love" they profess is a selfish feeling with no depth.

You see, real love isn't merely a feeling—it's a decision, an act of the will. Love determines to care about another person, even if that love is not reciprocated. It's a commitment that doesn't change or fade if the desired result is not gained. It's a sacrifice.

Real love is what God's Son, Jesus Christ, displayed for the world when He *chose* to sacrifice Himself for all of us. God did not have to give up His Son as a sacrifice for us, but He did! He knows that we don't deserve it. He knows the bad thoughts we entertain. He knows every awful thing about us, yet He loves us.

The Lord of absolutely everything, who knew us before we were born, has decided to love us. We mess up again and again; we fall short and still, He loves. God is committed to us, and He will faithfully forgive, unconditionally accept, and perfectly love us always.

Does that change your perspective on love? God has decided to love you! What have you decided?

What part of "Thou Shalt Not . . . " didn't you understand?
—GOD

*You have laid down precepts
that are to be fully obeyed.*

Psalm 119:4

Why did God give us a list of rules to follow? Why is the Bible so full of dos and don'ts? Is He some kind of big egomaniac who created us so that He would have someone to order around?

Look at it this way. Why doesn't a mother let her child touch a hot stove? Why doesn't a father let his kid run out into traffic? Rules like these don't always make sense to a child, but they are meant to protect—a way of ensuring that beloved child's safety and happiness.

Similarly, abiding by the commandments of the One who created us and the universe in which we live should provide heightened levels of protection, fulfillment, peace (both internal and external), and well-being. The quality of our lives is most often a product of our choices. The problem is that we don't always have the information or perspective we need to make proper choices. That's precisely why God, who loves us and greatly desires to see us succeed, has given us guidelines to live by.

If you have been viewing the Ten Commandments as the big stick God uses to beat His creation into submission, it may be time to shift your perspective. God is for you, not against you!

That "Love Thy Neighbor" thing . . . I meant that. —GOD

There is neither Jew nor Greek,
slave nor free, male nor female,
for you are all one in Christ Jesus.

Galatians 3:28

Martin Luther King Jr. said it well: "We must learn to live together like brothers or we will perish together like fools." And the key to living in harmony is to love your neighbors—all of them! Sure that's tough, because our tendency is to love only those who look like us, think like us, and act like us.

God made people different for a reason—just as He made more than one kind of flower, more than one kind of fruit, more than one kind of animal. We greatly limit our understanding and personal growth when we distance ourselves from other people simply because their skin is a different color, their customs seem odd and unfamiliar, or they live in a lower income bracket.

Want to add color and variety and understanding to your life? Want to please your Creator? Want to make the world a better place? The next time you have the opportunity, reach out to someone who doesn't look like you or live on your block.

God is the great equalizer. He celebrates the uniqueness and beauty of all His children. When you open your heart to God's love, He will help you see your neighbors as He sees them.

Keep using my name in vain, I'll make rush hour longer.
—GOD

You shall not misuse the name of the LORD your God, for the LORD will not hold anyone guiltless who misuses his name.

Exodus 20:7

Remember when you were a kid and classmates used your name to make fun of you? Maybe they rhymed your name with an unpleasant word or purposely mispronounced it. Maybe it was just the tone they used. No matter how old we are, we never seem to be able to completely forget those childhood taunts.

Why did they hurt so much? Perhaps it's because there's a lot in a name. Our possessions, our money, our job titles—all these can be taken from us. But our names stick. They were given to us by the people who love us. They identify who we are. Disrespect for our names shows disrespect for us and all we stand for.

The same is true with God. The Bible tells us that His is the "name above all names." Taking God's name in vain—using it irreverently, casually, or profanely—says something about our attitude toward Him. It tells Him that we do not respect or love Him. And if we fail to respect and love God, we fail to respect and love ourselves as His creation.

A solid respect for God will help you to instill respect for yourself and those around you. It is an essential ingredient for a successful life. Be wise, don't compromise!

Loved the wedding! Invite me to the marriage.
—GOD

*For this reason a man will leave his father
and mother and be united to his wife,
and they will become one flesh.*

Genesis 2:24

God invented relationships. He invented marriage. Can a project really be successful if we leave the Master Designer out of the picture?

Our heavenly Father understands better than we ever could what it takes to make a relationship work. He knows best what we need, and only when we submit to Him are we truly able to love each other. We can't really make our spouses happy on our own for the long haul.

A marriage not built on God's foundation is structurally flawed—destined to suffer cracks of selfishness and pride. It will be unable to withstand the storms and quakes of life. If you want a strong foundation for your marriage, check out the thirteenth chapter of 1 Corinthians in the New Testament of the Bible. Read about true love—the stuff from which strong marriages are made.

Remember, God used marriage to illustrate His relationship with His people. The Church is often called "the bride of Christ." The One who created us to be together first created us to be with Him. He wants what is best for us, and He wants to be involved in all of our human relationships, especially one as significant and life-changing as marriage. Invite Him into your marriage. His wisdom will be the best wedding gift of all.

"Big Bang Theory"? You've got to be kidding. —GOD

Through him all things were made; without him nothing was made that has been made. In him was life, and that life was the light of men.

John 1:3-4

Imagine a person walking into a museum in Florence, Italy. He or she gazes at the carefully, expertly crafted sculptures of great artists like Michelangelo—works of art that took months, even years to complete. Now imagine this person exclaiming, "Wow, I wonder what random series of accidents resulted in these beautiful sculptures?"

Logic and common sense dictate that the person in this scene is foolish. Intelligent design implies an intelligent designer. Great art requires a great artist. Yet, when it comes to the greatest artistic creation of all—the universe and all it contains—some people give the creative credit to a mysterious, cosmic "Big Bang."

You wouldn't see a windstorm whipping through a junkyard and assembling a 747, but some people insist that our world came to be through such an improbable accident. And never mind questions such as: Who created the energy for the Big Bang? Who created the materials that exploded? Who created the atmosphere in which this grand cosmic incident took place?

The Bible says that God created the universe and all that's in it. It was a cogent, purposeful act. Take a long look at the star-filled sky some evening. Then decide for yourself—the aftermath of an unlikely accident or the masterful hand of an artful Creator?

Will the road you're on get you to my place? —GOD

Our citizenship is in heaven. And we eagerly await a Savior from there, the Lord Jesus Christ.

Philippians 3:20

A young woman completing a job application came to the line asking for her "permanent address." She began to list her street and house number but paused for a moment. Then, with a small smile she wrote, "HEAVEN." She understood that Heaven is a real place—and the ultimate home of God's children.

No place on earth is truly home for those who belong to God's family. The Bible says that we are travelers—just passing through. Heaven is the ultimate, eternal destination for those who love God. In fact, their time on earth is like one small dot on a continuous, never-ending line.

Is God the landlord of your permanent home? If not, then the time is right to start investing in the future. Ask God to wash you clean and forgive your trespasses and sins so that you will be suitably clothed for Heaven's splendor. Ask Him to make you His child through the sacrifice of His Son. Ask Him to reserve a place for you, so that you can be with Him forever.

Heaven is the best home of all because God lives there. It is filled with hope and joy and peace and love, and it's forever. Start planning for your future *today!*

Follow me.
—GOD

*The world and its desires pass away, but
the man who does the will of God lives forever.*

1 John 2:17

What dreams and goals are you following? For many people, money and possessions are the treasure at the end of the rainbow. Americans, especially, have a possession obsession. Hand-held computers. Digital televisions. Cell phones with all the options. Sports cars. Money. Who wants to be a millionaire? Almost everybody, it seems.

Seeking material goals and comforts isn't inherently bad, of course. Neither is it wrong to strive to earn bonuses or profit sharing or build your retirement account. The problem is that materialism can become an all-consuming goal—a shallow, self-gratifying passion with no eternal significance.

God's Word teaches us to travel light. Slim wallets. Few possessions. In fact, Jesus Christ instructed His followers to take with them only the bare necessities when they set out on a journey. He reminded them not to be distracted by the glitter of shiny things.

In truth, the light of God's divine love is so brilliant that it makes everything else pale in comparison. That is the light we should run to, the light that brings happiness and fulfillment. Don't place your hopes in those things that don't last. Become a follower of God. Let Him guide you, and you will always be satisfied.

Need a marriage counselor? I'm available. —GOD

Cast your cares on the LORD
and he will sustain you.

Psalm 55:22

God could have used any number of analogies to illustrate His relationship with His followers: employer/employee, teacher/student, coach/athlete, and even master/slave. But the one He chose was groom/bride. Clearly, the relationship between husbands and wives is important to Him.

And since He invented marriage, God is intimately aware of its challenges and struggles. That's why He packed the Bible with advice on relationships and how to keep them strong and healthy. That's why He set out strategies for addressing and avoiding problems. That's why He instructed marriage partners to be humble, avoid demanding their own way, and make sacrifices for each other.

Remember that when you love, forgive, praise, care for, and celebrate your spouse, you are honoring a relationship God Himself created. You also receive a better understanding of how much God cherishes you and how much patience He practices in His relationship with you.

Come to God and express your marital frustrations and disappointments. He will listen and understand. He will show you how to restore life and love to your marriage relationship. He will also help you see how *you* can become a better marriage partner. God's advice is always wise. He is 100 percent fair. And the rates aren't bad, either.

Let's meet at my house Sunday before the game. —GOD

Let us not give up meeting together, as some are in the habit of doing, but let us encourage one another—and all the more as you see the Day approaching.

Hebrews 10:25

To have a close, rewarding relationship with God, you don't have to be perfect. But there is one requirement: You must be genuinely committed to the relationship. That includes spending time getting to know Him and His family.

Just as a person can't be "mostly married" or "somewhat pregnant," you cannot have a casual acquaintance with God. A relationship with the all-loving, all-powerful Creator of the universe just doesn't work that way. And part of building a meaningful relationship with God is spending time at His house with His people, the Church. Here, you can worship Him, learn how to live more effectively, hear how He is working in the lives of others, be supported by people who love Him and are committed to you for that very reason.

If you choose to avoid church, will God still love you? Of course. He loved you long before you were even aware of Him—and before the concept of church was invented. But if you truly want to grow close to God, to know Him as a friend, you need to spend some time at His house.

So what do you say? Will we be seeing you at the house this Sunday?

Tell the kids I love them.
—GOD

Whoever welcomes one of these little children in my name welcomes me; and whoever welcomes me does not welcome me but the one who sent me.

Mark 9:37

Some people think of God only as the Red Sea-parting, raising-the-dead power behind the universe. That certainly is a big part of who He is. But God also revealed Himself in the form of a helpless baby born in a Bethlehem manger two thousand years ago. The next time you hold a baby in your arms, imagine the Ruler of the universe crying with hunger or shivering from the cold.

God could have come to earth as a full-grown man or an invincible super-human hero. But He deliberately chose to begin His life as a child. He knows, from real experience, what it's like to be a kid. God the Son probably endured His share of skinned knees, nightmares, and bullies. No wonder the Bible is full of passages about how much God loves children. He knows how hard it is to be one.

One of the best ways to please the heavenly Father is to show love to His kids—regardless of their color, size, and shape. Physically or mentally challenged. Rich or poor. It's difficult for kids to believe that God cares for them if the adults they encounter don't reflect His heavenly love.

Next time you see one of God's little ones, be sure and pass along His love. He's depending on you.

Don't fear the future. I'm already there.
—GOD

There is surely a future hope for you,
and your hope will not be cut off.

Proverbs 23:18

It's human nature to fear the future. After all, none of us knows what's around the next bend. Life is a series of hills and valleys, sharp turns and bumpy roads. Sometimes we'll be sailing down an interstate highway, enjoying the scenery, when we hit an unexpected detour that takes us miles away from our destination. What if we make a wrong turn and get lost?

Don't worry. God's already been there before you. He knows where all the ruts and potholes and speed traps are. If you open His map book—the Bible—He'll show you the best route to take to avoid the worst roads.

You can trust God to lead you every step of the way. He knows the beginning and the end, as well as the middle of the journey. He will walk right by your side through every circumstance of life. And He will never leave you. There is nothing to fear when you are walking with Him.

There is one catch. You actually have to listen and let Him teach you. You'll wander around lost if you refuse to read the map or ask for directions. So trust Him to lead you in the right direction. All you have to do is ask!

Your secret's safe with me.
—GOD

Have faith in the LORD your God and you will be upheld.

2 Chronicles 20:20

Carolyn had become involved in activities that were not only morally wrong but also dangerous. She wanted to make a change but feared that telling her secret might expose her family to ridicule and shame. To keep the secret was painful—she needed a friend. In near desperation, she cried out to God, "I've got to talk to *someone!* Please send me someone I can trust?"

Almost before she had finished praying, the doorbell rang. When she opened the door, there stood the mother of one of her closest friends. Carolyn invited her in and almost immediately, she felt comfortable enough to pour out her heart.

Carolyn discovered her newfound friend had gone through similar struggles as a young person. She was able to give Carolyn the insight and courage she needed to regain control of her life. As they prayed together, Carolyn felt a profound peace fill her heart.

God knows all your secrets, your hidden fears, your desperate needs, and even your innermost thoughts. He loves you anyway. Ask for His help. Ask Him to send you someone who can help you find the answers you need—answers that will help you get your life back on track.

Some things break my heart too.
—GOD

If you spend yourselves in behalf of the hungry and satisfy the needs of the oppressed, then your light will rise in the darkness, and your night will become like the noonday.

Isaiah 58:10

Trevor was an average eleven-year-old when he saw a television special on Philadelphia's homeless. As he watched men and women huddling in alleys and under bridges, he felt compelled to do something. But what could a boy his age do? Finally, he convinced his parents to drive him from their well-to-do suburb into the heart of the city and let him give away his own pillow and blanket.

As they drove the streets of the downtown area, Trevor spotted a derelict camped on top of a subway grate. Trevor got out of the car and approached the man, offering his pillow and blanket. Amazed, the man looked into Trevor's eyes, smiled, and said, "God bless you."

That day, Trevor created a mission for himself. Soon, he and his father were on the streets again, this time with one of Trevor's mother's old coats. He returned again and again with clothing and hot food. When his own family ran out of clothing to give, Trevor canvassed his neighborhood. Word of his mission soon reached the local television stations, and the flow of gifts quickly became a flood.

The Bible teaches that God has great compassion for suffering humanity. When you respond with kindness to someone less fortunate, you can be sure that He sees and rejoices in your actions.[1]

I don't take *your* name in vain.
—GOD

You created my inmost being; you knit me together in my mother's womb. I praise you because I am fearfully and wonderfully made.

Psalm 139:13-14

Daniel Webster's eldest daughter was married to John Colby, considered to be one of the most wicked, godless men in his neighborhood when it came to impious behavior. He seemed to have no respect for God and often used His name in a derisive manner. Then Webster heard that Colby had undergone a change. He decided to call on him to see for himself.

On entering his daughter's home, he noticed a large-print Bible opened on a table. Colby had been reading it before he answered Webster's knock on the door. The first question Colby asked was, "Are you a Christian?" When he was assured of Webster's faith, he suggested that they kneel together and pray.

After the visit, Webster told a friend, "Here was a man as unlikely to be a Christian as any I have ever seen; and he has gone his godless way until now, with old age and habits hard to change! Yet now he is a penitent, trusting, humble believer!" God never gave up on John Colby.

You are precious to God. The Bible says that He knew you and loved you long before you were even aware of Him. No matter how you have treated Him in the past, He has never given up on you. Ask Him and find out for yourself.[2]

What would Jesus do? —GOD

Turn from evil and do good;
seek peace and pursue it.

Psalm 34:14

In *Up from Slavery,* Booker T. Washington describes meeting an ex-slave from Virginia:

"I found that this man had made a contract with his master, two or three years previous to the Emancipation Proclamation. The slave was to be permitted to buy himself, by paying so much per year for his body; and while he was paying for himself, he was to be permitted to labor where and for whom he pleased.

"Finding that he could secure better wages in Ohio, he went there.

"When freedom came, the man was still in debt to his master some three hundred dollars. Notwithstanding that the Emancipation Proclamation freed him from any obligation to his master, this black man walked back to where his old master lived in Virginia and placed the last dollar, with interest, in his hands.

"In talking to me about this, the man told me that he knew that he did not have to pay his debt but that he had given his word to his master, and he had never broken his word. He felt that he could not enjoy his freedom until he had fulfilled his promise."

You can depend on it. God always keeps His word! Do you?

You're precious to me!
—GOD

How wide and long and high and deep is the love of Christ.

Ephesians 3:18

The love of God is difficult to comprehend on every level. Why would the great and mighty Creator of the universe care about us—no more than pinpoints from the cosmic perspective? We may never be able to answer that question fully, but what does it matter—the fact is He does!

Not only does He love us, but the Bible says He loves us individually, unconditionally, gently, intimately, eternally, closely, warmly, tenderly, protectively, and kindly. We are told that His love is deep and fervent. He is constantly watching over us, and we are always on His mind.

Many reject God's love because they don't feel they deserve it. But the Bible tells us that God knows we aren't deserving. His love is a gift—freely given rather than something that has been earned. He has made it available to every person—adult or child, man or woman. And it's free, though not cheap. God paid a very high price when He reached out to redeem us—the life of His only Son!

Have you experienced the love of God in a personal way? If not, open your heart and let Him fill it. Reach out and take hold of God's wonderful gift. It will change your life forever.

Do I have an offer for you!
—GOD

"I know the plans I have for you," declares the LORD,
*"plans to prosper you and not to harm you,
plans to give you hope and a future."*

Jeremiah 29:11

On a bleak winter morning, Jim felt overwhelmed by a sense of failure. He kept thinking, *My life is worthless. I don't fit in.* He was forty-three years old. Alcohol was destroying his life, and now, he had lost his job. Jim didn't see that he had any future. Then he remembered Ted.

Ted was Jim's AA sponsor, a crusty straight-talking farmer. Jim drove to Ted's house and found him sitting by his wood-burning stove. Ted seemed genuinely pleased to see Jim and began telling him how things were going on the farm. Finally, Jim began to pour out his heart to Ted, rehearsing years of disappointments, hurts, and failures.

"I know things seem hopeless right now," Ted told him, "but God has a wonderful plan for your life. Give Him all your disappointments and failures, and He will give you a sense of peace deeper than any you have ever known."

"God wouldn't want me," Jim responded. "My life is a mess. I have nothing to offer Him."

"But He does want you," said Ted. "He wants you just the way you are. You give Him your mess, and He will give you His peace. It's an amazing offer."

No matter what condition your life is in, the same offer is available to you.

When I said, "I love you," did you believe me? —GOD

God demonstrates his own love for us in this: While we were still sinners, Christ died for us.

Romans 5:8

A minister told of a certain family in his church who had waited a long time for a child. The couple was overjoyed when at last a son was born to them, but they were crushed to learn that he had a severe handicap. Without warning, the boy would be thrown into violent seizures.

Whenever the church doors were open, this family could be found in attendance, the father always holding his precious child on his lap. One Sunday, the boy experienced a particularly hard seizure. The father held him firmly to his chest as he walked to the back of the church, gently whispering comforting words into the boy's ears as he went. There was no hint of embarrassment or frustration on that father's face—only calm, deep, abiding love.

That is a picture of our heavenly Father's love for us. In spite of our deep imperfections, He is not embarrassed to call us His children. He tenderly holds us through the deepest, hardest part of our struggles and whispers words of assurance and encouragement while He clutches us to Himself and supports us with His loving care.

God loves you unconditionally, and He longs to let you know. You can believe it!

Relax.
I'm in control.
—GOD

Do not be anxious about anything, but in everything, by prayer and petition, with thanksgiving, present your requests to God.

Philippians 4:6

After two failed attempts to land, a balloonist panicked. Knowing he had only half of one tank of fuel left, he frantically scanned the thick woods for a spot to attempt another landing. Nearly paralyzed with fear, he cried out to God, "Help me. Take control of this situation. Lord, find me a safe place to land!" With that prayer, a feeling of calm came over him. His fingers unclenched, and he felt a wave of peace.

A few seconds later, the balloonist spotted a small clearing directly ahead—and in it, two of the biggest bulls he had ever seen. He held on tightly as the basket hit the ground, tipped over, and was dragged for about fifty yards.

To his amazement, the bulls seemed oblivious to all the commotion. As his ground crew came racing toward him, one of them said, "How were you able to keep the balloon under control?" The balloonist laughed to himself for he knew the truth. He had landed safely because he had given up control to God.

Does your life seem to be out of control? Ask God for help. He's done a great job with the universe. Being invited to help you get a grip on your life will be His pleasure. Remember, He loves you![3]

I build great homes.
—GOD

As God's chosen people, holy and dearly loved, clothe yourselves with compassion, kindness, humility, gentleness and patience.

Colossians 3:12

One of the most interesting of all natural phenomena is the nightly return of the "fairie penguins" to their rookery in the sand dunes off southern Australia.

These penguins, only about a foot in height, swim for days, even weeks, fishing for food. As dusk approaches, one or more groups of fairie penguins return home. As if the waves are spurting ink onto the sand, they spill out of the surf, then assemble together in tight clusters, gathering the courage to cross the naked sands. They make a bold dash for the dunes, hopping up and over any obstacles they encounter, each penguin hobbling toward its nest on a well-worn, tiny path.

Once at home, each penguin greets his or her "spouse" at the opening of the sandy cave. They peck at each other as if kissing. Fairie penguins usually mate for life, and they take equal responsibility for nurturing their young. Amazingly, God has instilled in these creatures the truth that a house also should be a home—a place where love, respect, and fellowship reside, and where man and wife work as a team.

God is in the business of building homes. If your house is just a house and needs some remodeling to make it a home, invite Him in to do the work.

Have you told me lately that you love me?
—GOD

"Do you love me?" . . . *"Feed my sheep."*

John 21:17

Many years ago, on a bitterly cold day in February, a little boy was standing barefoot in front of a shoe store in New York City. A woman riding up the street in a beautiful carriage saw him and ordered her driver to stop. She alighted from her carriage and quickly went to the boy. "My little fellow, why are you looking so earnestly in that window?"

"I was asking God to give me a pair of shoes," he replied, shivering. The woman took him by the hand and went into the store. She asked the proprietor for half-a-dozen pairs of socks. She also asked for a basin of water and a towel. When he brought them to her, she took the boy to the back of the store, removed her gloves, knelt down, washed his grimy feet, and dried them with the towel.

She then had him put on a pair of socks. Returning to the front of the store, she bought him a pair of shoes. As they parted she said, "I hope, my little fellow, that you are more comfortable."

He caught her hand and with tears in his eyes replied to her, "Are you God's wife?" If you love God, it will show.

Give me
your worries.
I'll be up all
night anyway.
—GOD

He will never let me stumble, slip or fall.
For he is always watching, never sleeping.

Psalm 121:3-4 TLB

When Walter Wangerin was a boy, he told all of his friends that his father was the strongest man alive. Then came the day when Wally climbed to the top of the backyard cherry tree. A storm blew up suddenly, and Wally was trapped. Wind ripped through the tree with such velocity that it was all Wally could do to hang on to a branch about ten feet above the ground. "Daddy!" he shouted, and instantly his father appeared. "Jump," he yelled up to Wally. "Jump, and I'll catch you."

Wally was frozen in fear. His big, strong dad looked quite small and frail down there on the ground. Wally thought, *If I jump and Dad doesn't catch me, I'll hit the ground and die!* "No!" he screamed back.

At that very moment the limb Wally was clinging to cracked at the trunk. Wally didn't jump—he *fell*—straight into Dad's ready arms. Crying and trembling, Wally realized that his Dad *was* strong after all. Up to that point, it had only been a theory. Now it was a reality.

Give God all your worries. Day or night, He is always waiting patiently for you to let them drop safely into His strong arms. No matter what you are facing, He is more than strong enough to handle it.[4]

Live for me;
I died for you.
—GOD

"He who believes in me will live, even though he dies; and whoever lives and believes in me will never die."

John 11:25-26

An old farmer in northern India brought his goods to sell at the village bazaar. Among the items was a whole covey of quail. In order to keep them together, he tied a string around one leg of each bird and attached the strings to a ring, which fit over a stick driven into the ground. The farmer exercised the birds by training them to walk around and around in a circle.

For most of the day, the farmer had no offers on the quail. Then along came a devout religious man of the highest Hindu caste. He had great reverence for all of life and felt deep, profound compassion for the little birds walking in a never-ending circle.

The religious man asked the farmer the price of the quail and then offered to buy them all. The farmer was elated, but to his surprise the holy man handed him the money and said, "Cut the strings from their legs and set them free!" The farmer did as he was told. After all, the birds were no longer his—he had been paid for them.

God's own Son, Jesus Christ, has purchased your freedom. The price He paid—His very life! Now you are free to become all God intended you to be.

Are you talking to me? —GOD

Answer me when I call to you,
O my righteous God. Give me relief from
my distress; be merciful to me and hear my prayer.

Psalm 4:1

After two long days of lying on the ocean floor in their disabled submarine, the sub's crew members received orders from their commanding officer to sing the following hymn:

Abide with me! Fast falls the eventide.
The darkness deepens—Lord, with me abide!
When other helpers fail and comforts flee,
Help of the helpless, oh, abide with me!

After the hymn had been sung, the commander explained to his men that the hymn was his prayer for them and that he hoped it would hold the same meaning for them as it did for him. He then explained that based upon the best information he had, they did not have long to live. There was little or no hope of outside aid, because any searchers who might be on the surface did not know the vessel's position.

Sedatives were distributed to the men to quiet their nerves. One sailor, overcome at the commander's news, fainted. As he swooned, he fell against a piece of equipment, setting in motion the surfacing mechanism that had been jammed! The submarine rose to the surface safely and soon made port.

If you have hit bottom in life, talk to God about it. He is always listening, and He will surely answer you when you reach out to Him for help.[5]

Safe sex? It's called marriage.
—GOD

*Marriage should be honored by all,
and the marriage bed kept pure.*

Hebrews 13:4

In *Sin, Sex, and Self-Control*, Norman Vincent Peale writes: "Martha took the kids away to the mountains for a month, so I was a summer bachelor. And about midway through that month, I met a girl, a beautiful girl looking for excitement. She made it clear that I had a green light—so for one weekend I put my conscience in mothballs and arranged a meeting with her for Saturday night."

Peale said that he woke up Saturday morning, put on his swimming trunks, and took a walk on the beach to clear his head. As he walked, a strange thing began to happen.

He said, "I felt as if I were outside myself, looking at myself through a kind of fog that was gradually clearing. And suddenly I knew that what I had been planning for that evening was so wrong, so out of key with my standards and my loyalties and the innermost me that it was out of the question." He canceled the date.

God's commandments have come to be viewed as stone tablets filled with restrictions on our fun. In truth, they were given to protect, rather than prohibit, our happiness. God wants you to be truly safe—safe to enjoy a happy and fulfilled life.[6]

Miss you.
—GOD

You turned away from God, your Creator;
you forgot the Mighty Rock, the source of your life.

Deuteronomy 32:18 CEV

Imagine for a moment that someone you love comes to you and asks to borrow a small sum of money. You no doubt would lend it gladly, in part because of the close relationship you share.

Now imagine that this same person continues to come to you, asking for loans, food, clothing, the use of your car, and a place to stay. At the same time, let's imagine that your friend approaches you only when he or she needs something—no time for anything more.

While you do love this person, you would probably begin to feel that something is wrong. It's not the asking but the attitude. No one wants to feel they are significant only as a source of goods and services.

So often we come to God with our request list in hand—"God, please do this . . ." or "God, I want. . . ." God delights in answering our prayers and providing for our needs, but He wants us to think of Him as more than a big "vending machine" in the sky. His desire is for us to know Him personally and spend time with Him daily, enjoying the wonders of His loving presence.

Have you ever considered approaching God just to be sociable? Now might be a good time to start.

Sleepless? A clear conscience is a great pillow.
—GOD

I will maintain my righteousness and never let go of it; my conscience will not reproach me as long as I live.

Job 27:6

In *My Utmost for His Highest*, Oswald Chambers wrote, "Conscience is that ability within me that attaches itself to the highest standard I know and then continually reminds me of what the standard demands that I do. It is the eye of the soul that looks out either toward God or toward what we regard as the highest standard. The question is, will I obey?

"God does not speak with a voice like thunder—His voice is so gentle that it is easy for us to ignore. And the only thing that keeps our conscience sensitive to Him is the habit of being open to God on the inside. When you begin to debate, stop immediately. Don't ask, 'Why can't I do this?' You are on the wrong track. There is no debating possible once your conscience speaks. Whatever it is—drop it, and see that you keep your inner vision clear."

When we do things that we sense instinctively are wrong, we unleash a storm of conflict and emotion within our own souls. We lose our way.

Your conscience is a gift from God, designed to help you build a life of peace and contentment. Have you been listening to that still, small voice within?[7]

If you must have the last word, make it "Sorry." —GOD

If you are angry, don't sin by nursing your grudge. Don't let the sun go down with you still angry—get over it quickly.

Ephesians 4:26 TLB

Anger is destructive. Physicians know it. Marriage counselors know it. Law enforcement officers know it. Anger can cause ulcers, migraines, and heart attacks. It can destroy marriages and relationships. Our prisons are full of angry men and women who had to have the last word and resorted to violence.

That's why God warned us not to hold grudges. Even when you suffer in silence and turn a cold shoulder to a neighbor, a coworker, or spouse, the anger eats at you like a cancer. It's insatiable. It needs regular feedings of hatred and bitterness—emotions that are the antithesis of God's loving-kindness. It's for our own good that God asks us to treat one another with love, honor, and respect. He knows we're going to get angry sometimes, but He has given us self-control and those beautiful words, "I'm sorry."

Are you angry? Do you resent the way you've been treated by others? Let it go. You'll never be able to look forward to those things God has for you if you're always looking at the past. Or have you hurt someone else? Apologize and go on with your life. They may not forgive you, but God will. Pray about those bridges you know need building, and ask God to help you build a few today.

I don't play favorites.
—GOD

[God] is not partial to princes, nor does He regard the rich more than the poor, for they all are the work of His hands.

Job 34:19 AMP

The world plays favorites. We have our favorite football teams, our favorite movie stars, our favorite politicians, and our favorite friends. We like to be part of the "in" crowd. We separate ourselves from those people we don't think are quite as good as we are and form cliques with those we think are worthy of our time.

But God doesn't play favorites! He doesn't prefer the college president to the janitor, or the nuclear scientist to the waitress. He loves them all. That's His nature. So what if you grew up on the wrong side of the tracks? So what if you still live there? You're just as important to Him as anyone else.

God does have some requirements, however. He hates pride and arrogance, so He insists that we come to Him with a humble and honest heart. He hates sin, so He requires that we first discard our sinfulness and ask to be clothed in the white robes of forgiveness.

God wants to have a relationship with you. That may surprise you, but it's true! He loves you as much as He loves each other person—with all His heart. Won't you open your heart and life to Him? You will always be glad you did!

When it comes to eternity, three things matter: location, location, location.
—GOD

"What good will it be for a man if he gains the whole world, yet forfeits his soul?"

Matthew 16:26

Sadhu Sundar Singh was born into an Indian family of high caste. When he became a Christian and told his parents of his decision to follow Christ, they said, "You have broken caste." They immediately banished him from their home.

It was the wet season, and the rain was coming down hard as he left his home, clad in only his insubstantial Indian robes. He sat under a nearby tree all night, soaked to the skin. He said that he felt so radiantly happy, however, that he forgot any physical discomfort. He had the freedom to travel throughout the region telling the Gospel story.

He became known as the apostle of India. Once he went into Tibet, where he was arrested, put into a pit, and branded with irons. He bore those scars the rest of his life. While speaking in England, he said, "I am going back to do what I have done. I am quite aware of the cost." Sometime after his return to India, he disappeared and appears to have suffered a martyr's death.

Singh willingly moved from "high caste" in India into a "servant's caste." Why? Because He believed that the best life this world has to offer could not compare to the promise of eternity in God's presence. Where will you spend eternity?[8]

Red, brown, yellow, black, and white— they are precious in my sight. —GOD

"I assure you that whatever you did for the humblest of my brothers you did for me."

Matthew 25:40 PHILLIPS

God created a world of infinite variety. There are millions of different animal species, flowers, and plants. No two snowflakes are alike. No two fingerprints are alike. No two voices are alike. The night sky is blanketed with stars, comets, and planets. God must love diversity.

If God's imagination can create such a fantastic universe, why would we think people would all come in the same color? We are spiritual beings on the inside. But on the outside, some of us are white hothouse orchids; some are yellow daisies and bright marigolds, while some are velvety purple petunias. Yet it takes all of us to make up this beautiful garden we call home.

Still, many continue to let the color of our skin polarize and separate us from one another. Many people of all colors continue to allow hatred and animosity to drive them to commit shameful acts. We have even endured wars because we were unable to see that a diversity of color is a gift from a loving and creative God.

Reach out a hand of friendship to someone of a different skin color. You may find that you have more in common than you could ever have imagined.

Got questions? I'm the answer.
—GOD

Jesus told him, "I am the Way—yes, and the Truth and the Life. No one can get to the Father except by means of me."

John 14:6 TLB

People are full of questions: Does God really exist? Can He hear my prayers? Am I good enough to get into Heaven? Yes, yes, and . . . sorry . . . no. Yes, God is real. Yes, He hears your prayers. And no, you're not good enough to get into Heaven. None of us are. But don't panic; there's an answer for that too.

Ever eavesdropped at a funeral? The conversation usually goes something like this: "So-and-so was such a good person. He'd give you the shirt off his back"—as if that guaranteed a one-way ticket to Heaven. People have the impression that God is adding up all their good deeds on a giant calculator, and when He reaches some magical number, the pearly gates automatically swing open.

It doesn't work that way. Jesus told His disciples not to worry because He was going away to prepare a place for them. Then He explained He was going away to His Father's house—Heaven—and the only way to get there was through Him.

Nobody's good enough, smart enough, cute enough, or successful enough to be acceptable to a just and holy God. But when He looks at us through the eyes of Jesus, we become pleasing in His sight. Jesus is the answer!

Feeling down? Just look up. —GOD

Praise the LORD! Oh, give thanks to the LORD, for He is good! For His mercy endures forever.

Psalm 106:1 NKJV

Although they may not have known its title or by whom it was painted, most people have seen a copy of *The Song of the Lark*, a famous painting by the French artist Jules Breton.

The painting depicts a peasant girl on her way to the field for a hard day's work. Suddenly, it appears, she has heard the sound of a lark. Breton captures her upturned face, alive with hope and joy, thrilled to hear the lilting beauty of the lark's sweet song. From her dress, she is obviously just another peasant girl with a difficult, workaday life. But Breton captures something of her inner soul—a human being glorying in one of nature's loveliest voices, a person enriched by the beauty of God's creation.

Interestingly, the painting has no image of a bird in it. The lark that gives rise to such pleasure is unseen.

And so it is with God. We cannot see Him with our physical eyes. Nevertheless, we can feel His presence and hear His words of comfort, admonition, and encouragement. We do see Him moving in the circumstances. Though unseen, He adds joy, hope, meaning, and purpose to our day-to-day lives.

He is singing a song especially for *you* today. Look up and listen![9]

Got grace?
—GOD

My grace is sufficient for thee: for my strength is made perfect in weakness.

2 Corinthians 12:9 KJV

Christian and Holocaust survivor, Corrie ten Boom, often recounted a conversation she had with her father. Even as a child, Corrie sensed the dangers of Hitler's message of hatred and genocide. They were not Jews, but Corrie knew her family would not stand by silently as their Jewish neighbors and friends disappeared into the night.

Fearing the unspeakable, Corrie asked her father if God would protect them and if so, how. She recalls that her father responded with the following analogy. "If you were taking a trip, Corrie, you would not need your ticket until you arrived at the station ready to board the train. At the very moment you need God's grace, it will be poured out on you—enough to see you through any circumstance."

In the end, the horrors of Nazism did turn Corrie's life upside down and changed it forever. And yet, Corrie often stated that her father's words were true. Each time she faced an impossibly difficult situation, God's grace sustained her with hope and courage.

You may never face circumstances as severe as those Corrie ten Boom endured. But, you may be just as apprehensive about what the future holds. Reach out for God's grace. He promises that it will be there when you need it—every time you need it.

Need a lifeline?
—GOD

The Lord is faithful, and he will strengthen and protect you from the evil one.

2 Thessalonians 3:3

On a remote farm in California, a young mother was alone with her three children. The children had been swimming in the family pool when she suddenly noticed her two-and-a-half-year-old son lying lifeless on the bottom. She dove in and pulled him out as quickly as she could.

Just at that moment, a neighboring farmer came by. He immediately began to apply CPR. After several minutes, the child stirred. The mother and the farmer took him to the nearest hospital for examination, and the doctors assured them that the little boy had suffered no brain damage.

In the days following, as people heard of the child's rescue, several commented to the mother and father, "You sure were lucky!" The father said to his pastor, "When people said that to me, I replied, 'It wasn't luck at all. My wife and daughter were praying while the farmer was working on my son. He survived because God intervened.'"

When you find yourself in the midst of a crisis, don't cross your fingers and depend on luck. Put your trust in God. Cry out to Him for a lifeline. He will meet you right where you are, in the moment of your need.[10]

Darwin says to tell you that he was wrong.

—GOD

God created man in his own image,
in the image of God He created him;
male and female he created them.

Genesis 1:27

When Darwin's "theory of evolution" was first introduced into our public schools, it was considered to be just that—a theory. These days, evolution is taught as a foregone conclusion.

Most thinking people would agree that some form of evolutionary process is at work on the earth. However, it's silly to suggest that the theory posited by Darwin eliminates the possibility of a creative God who authored the universe. If we follow the "evolutionary trail" backward to its farthest point, we are still left to wonder, *How did it all begin?*

The discussion about what came from what will always find its way back to the hand of God. So why does the discussion rage on? Because distancing ourselves from our Creator relieves us of the responsibility of responding to Him. It allows us to feel like the captains of our own ships, owing our existence to a simple series of accidents.

What a shame! For when we deny our Creator, we deny the song that is embedded in our hearts. It cuts us off from our true identity and leaves us floundering in a sea of insecurity and uncertainty. No matter what you might think about the "theory of evolution," God predates it. Open your heart to see your Creator and His great love for you!

Going my way?
—GOD

*"Small is the gate and narrow the road
that leads to life, and only a few find it."*

Matthew 7:14

Many years ago when Egyptian troops conquered Nubia, a regiment of soldiers was crossing the Nubian desert with an Arab guide.

Recognizing that they had limited water and were suffering from great thirst, the soldiers were deceived by the appearance of a beautiful lake on the horizon. They insisted that their guide take them to its banks. The guide, who knew the desert well, knew that what they saw was just a mirage. In vain, he told the men that the lake was not real. He refused to lose precious time by wandering from the designated course.

Angry words led to blows and in the end, the soldiers killed the guide. As they moved toward the lake, it receded into the distance. Finally, they recognized their error—the lake was only burning sand. Raging thirst and horrible despair engulfed the soldiers. Without their guide, the pathless desert was a mystery. They had been sure they knew what was best. Instead they had sealed their own fate.

You may be certain you know what's right for your life, what will bring you happiness and success. You may in fact be so sure that you feel you don't need God's help. Don't deceive yourself. Only God knows the beginning from the end and every step along the way.[11]

Remember that pretty sunset? I painted it just for you.
—GOD

He has made everything beautiful in its time.

Ecclesiastes 3:11

A businessman working in the Orient happened to meet a blind man from Belgium, who sat next to him during dinner and a show. The man said, "I'd love it if you'd describe a little of what you see." The businessman happily agreed.

The blind man asked him to describe the musicians, which the businessman had failed to note, and then to describe their instruments. "What do our fellow tourists look like?" the blind man asked. The businessman described two in detail: an elderly Japanese woman and a blond Scandinavian boy. When the show began, he described the dancers, their golden four-inch fingernails, and their elegant movements.

The businessman later commented: "I discovered colors, patterns, and designs of local costumes; the texture of skin under soft lights; the movement of long, black Asian hair as elegant heads angled to the music; the intense expressions of the musicians as they played; even the flashing white smile of our waitress." At the close of the evening, the blind man said, "How beautifully you saw everything for me."

Ask God to open your eyes and help you see the intricate beauty and detail of the world around you as you have never seen it before. It's His gift to you, and you have only begun to realize its splendor.[12]

It's not too late to be what you might have been.
—GOD

Forget the former things; do not dwell on the past. . . . I am making a way in the desert and streams in the wasteland.

Isaiah 43:18-19

Have you ever tried to reroute a stream by building a dam across the water with rocks and stones? Have you ever built a mud dam to collect the flowing water into a pool? These efforts were never completely successful, were they? The stones eventually give way to the rush of water and the mud dam washes downstream.

Every day we meet challenges that can potentially divert us and even temporarily defeat God's purpose in our lives. Failures, poor choices, or fear may derail us for a time. But if we turn to God and ask for His help, these obstacles will never permanently defeat His plan for us.

What are you facing today? A life impeded by mistakes, circumstances, even the harm someone else has inflicted on you? Do you feel you will never fulfill your dreams? You must not give up!

God is the author of miracles. He can take a life—no matter how broken—and make of it a beautiful and uniquely new creation. He will push away the stones and allow life-giving water to flow once more. Come to Him right now. It's never too late for you to become all that God created you to be.

Proud parent of the Savior of the world.
—GOD

*This is my Son, whom I love; with him
I am well pleased. Listen to him!*

Matthew 17:5

The vast majority of households in our nation tune in to the national and local news at least once during the day. While we often decry the negative messages of most news stories, we seem addicted to hearing more and more. The Gospel shines in sharp contrast.

The word "gospel" is derived from an early Anglo-Saxon word "godspel." It means "good tidings" and later also took on the meaning "God-story" or the story of God's love shown to us through the sacrifice of His Son, Jesus Christ.

So when you are watching the daily news and begin to feel overwhelmed by the crime, racial tension, war, conflict, catastrophes, accidents, disease, and lawlessness, look upward and thank God that He did not leave us in this world without hope. He sent His only Son to help us navigate the icy waters of this life and give us the certainty of a future in His presence, free from wickedness and evil.

Have you opened your heart to greet the Savior of the world, God's precious Son? The Bible says that God's Son, Jesus Christ, stands at the door of your heart and knocks. If you open the door and let Him come in, you will never be alone again to face the confusion and turmoil of this life. That's Good News!

Hell:
Don't go there.
—GOD

*The memory of the righteous will be a blessing,
but the name of the wicked will rot.*

Proverbs 10:7

A rather unsavory character was being buried one day. He had never been anywhere near a place of worship in his entire life, and the services were being conducted by a minister who had never heard of him. Caught up in the moment, the minister became carried away with the occasion. He poured on great praise for the departed man in his desire to bring as much comfort as possible to the family.

As the preacher lamented the great loss of this father, husband, and boss, the man's widow, whose expression had grown more and more puzzled, nudged her son and whispered, "Go up there and make sure it's Papa."

Regardless of your station in life or the material possessions you may amass, the day will come when your life will end. Will you leave behind a legacy of hate, immorality, and faithlessness? Or will you endow those who have known you with love, faithfulness, and hope? And where will you spend eternity?

Today is the day of opportunity. You may not have tomorrow. Decide today to turn your back on hell and your eyes toward Heaven. Live your life in such a way that even the kind words of a stranger will ring true in the ears of those who knew you. Begin now![13]

What's your hurry? —GOD

Be still, and know that I am God.

Psalm 46:10

The only way we can know God is by *experiencing Him.* Many of those experiences come as we take time to listen quietly for His voice.

Søren Kierkegaard noted that most of us are "so busy," we are unwilling to wait patiently for God. We might consider an appointment with a hairdresser to be productive time, but when God lays claim to our time, we balk. Rather than spend time with God and allow ourselves to bask in His presence and soak up His love, we manufacture substitutes— things to do to take the place of simply *being* with Him. Even the admirable activities of good works and Bible study can keep us from resting quietly with Him.

Like any other relationship, experiencing God takes both quality and quantity time and a willingness to listen to Him. There is no substitute for either. Like any other relationship, we must be willing to make a conscious investment of time and effort.

Slow down and listen for God's voice today. He speaks often to each of us deep within the recesses of our hearts and minds. The trouble is that most people are moving too fast to receive the transmission. You may be surprised to hear what you've been missing.[14]

Just where is this relationship going, anyway? —GOD

Now, dear children, continue in him, so that when he appears we may be confident and unashamed before him at his coming.

1 John 2:28

Have you ever watched a potter begin to shape a vessel? He begins by carefully wetting his hands, selecting his clay, and placing it on the wheel. As he or she begins to turn the wheel, the lumps in the clay are revealed. Spinning the wheel faster, he smoothes out the lumps, and the clay begins to take on an unruffled appearance. This is just the first step, however.

The potter then shapes the mass of clay so that it is perfectly aligned with the very center of the wheel. This requires both strength and a loving, delicate touch. This "centering" is the most important step in the preparation process because it gives the piece strength and integrity.

Walking in relationship with God is much like the potter and the clay. When He first enters our lives, we are like a piece of clay with many lumps. As we learn to trust Him and let Him mold our lives, however, we become perfectly aligned with His true purpose for our lives. Soon we are transformed into beautiful, strong vessels.

God wants to make a beautiful vessel from the clay that is your life. Don't neglect your relationship with Him. Open your heart and allow Him to mold and shape you until you are all He created you to be.

Leggo your ego.
—GOD

Pride goes before destruction,
a haughty spirit before a fall.

Proverbs 16:18

Antonio Salieri, an ambitious, albeit mediocre, eighteenth-century composer offers this prayer in the popular film on Mozart's life, *Amadeus:*

"Lord, make me a great composer. Let me celebrate Your glory through music and be celebrated myself. Make me famous throughout the world, dear God; make me immortal. After I die, let people speak my name forever with love for what I wrote. In return I will give You my chastity, my industry, my deep humility, my life."

When it became obvious to the superficially pious Salieri that he would never be as gifted as the roguish Wolfgang Amadeus Mozart, he became insanely jealous of Mozart and plotted to destroy him. He also turned from God. As far as Salieri was concerned, God had betrayed him. He had failed to answer his prayer. In a very powerful scene in the movie, he takes a crucifix from the wall of his room and places it into the fire.

Don't let ego and pride keep you from the love of God. No matter what you may have planned for your life, God's plan is grander still. Put away selfishness and cruel ambition. God will give you a life of fulfillment and peace in exchange.[15]

Have you read *my* top 10 list lately? —GOD

Fear God and keep his commandments,
for this is the whole duty of man.

Ecclesiastes 12:13

In an extensive opinion survey, *The Day America Told the Truth*, James Patterson and Peter Kim reported some startling findings:

- Only thirteen percent saw all Ten Commandments as binding and relevant.

- Ninety-one percent lied regularly, both at work and home.

- Most workers admitted to goofing off an average of seven hours a week.

- About half of the workforce admitted they regularly called in sick even when they felt well.

When they were asked what they would be willing to do for ten million dollars, 25 percent said they would abandon their families, 23 percent would be prostitutes for a week, and 7 percent would murder a stranger!

God's commandments were never meant to enslave us. They were meant to guide us away from chaos and lawlessness. They were meant to teach us how to live peacefully and safely with our neighbors. They were meant to keep us from the consequences of destructive behaviors.

God's commandments were intended to bring order and happiness to our lives rather than to restrict our freedom. If you haven't read God's commandments, open up the Bible and take a look. You will find an outline for successful living—a gift from a loving Father.

Knees knocking? Try kneeling on them.
—GOD

From the depths . . . I called for help,
and you listened to my cry.

Jonah 2:2

In recent years, nearly every community in the United States has been equipped with a 911 emergency phone system. The newest versions of this system are state of the art. All a person has to do is dial those three numbers and he is instantly connected to a dispatcher.

The dispatcher's computer screen identifies the number from which the call is being made, the address, and the name for whom the telephone number is listed. The system is simultaneously connected to the police department, fire department, and paramedics. A person using the 911 system doesn't even need to utter a word in order for help to be activated and dispatched to the scene.

God has long had His own 911 system—a system more foolproof, failproof, and faithful than anything man can hope to design. When we dial "911" prayers, we are sometimes hysterical, or we don't know the right words to convey the deep need we feel. But God hears.

God already knows your name and all about your circumstances. He knows the precise answer to your problem even before you ask. When you are facing fearful circumstances, call out to God. His help will be on the way the moment you speak His name.

Like Father, like Son.
—GOD

In Christ all the fullness of
the Deity lives in bodily form.

Colossians 2:9

No matter how we might try to deny it at times, we all exhibit many of the characteristics of our human mothers and fathers. Perhaps it is the color of our eyes, our hair, the size of our feet, or a certain temperament or personality. Even though God has created each one of us as a unique individual, He has also chosen to link us inextricably to our parents by placing within us our parent's genetic imprint.

The Bible says that Jesus Christ is God's only "begotten" Son and that He has been with Him from the beginning of time and before. In the same way we are linked to our parents, Jesus is linked to His Father—GOD.

If you wonder what God is really like or long to understand Him person to person, read the four Gospels, which describe the life of Jesus. You will soon begin to appreciate and understand God in an entirely new way. No longer will He seem unknowable and incomprehensible. As an insightful five-year-old once said, "Jesus is God with skin on."

Open your heart to Jesus and you will be embracing both the Father and the Son. You will never be the same!

No one ever choked on swallowed pride.
—GOD

A man's pride brings him low, but a man of lowly spirit gains honor.

Proverbs 29:23

Dutch author and priest Henri Nouwen admits in his book *In the Name of Jesus* that he came to a place where he felt as if his life was in a rut. On the surface, it would seem that Nouwen had it made. He possessed an impressive résumé in a noble field of study. But after twenty-five years in the priesthood, he found himself praying poorly, living a life isolated from people, and preoccupied with doubts.

Finally, Nouwen asked God if he should leave his prestigious role as a distinguished professor. The answer was clear. God led Nouwen to the L'Arche Community for the Mentally Handicapped. In Nouwen's words, "God said, 'Go and live among the poor of spirit, and they will heal you.'" So he did.

In his new role, Nouwen faced numerous lessons, some painful, a few humiliating, but in all, he learned humility, compassion, and caring. Pride in his own accomplishments could have kept him from finding the fulfillment he was so desperately seeking. Nouwen's willingness to swallow his pride and answer God's call led him ultimately to buried treasure.

If you lack purpose and fulfillment, turn your life over to God. Don't let pride stand in your way.

You look like you could use a faith-lift.
—GOD

This is the victory that has
overcome the world, even our faith.

1 John 5:4

There may be no better feeling in the world than the joy of winning a race you were never expected to win. Just ask Jenny Spangler. She won the women's marathon at the U.S. Olympic trials in 1996, earning the right to compete at the summer Olympic Games in Atlanta, Georgia.

At the time of the trials, Spangler was qualifier number sixty-one, which meant that sixty runners had entered the race with faster times than hers. She had set an American junior record in the marathon during college but left the sports scene after a stress fracture dashed her hopes in the Olympic trials of 1984. No one thought she could maintain a winning pace when she passed the leaders at the sixteen-mile mark.

The favorites in that amazing marathon expected Spangler to fade, but she never did. Somewhere inside herself, she found the courage and stamina to finish strong. She took home first prize and won a place on the Olympic team.

Does the day ahead of you look as grueling as a marathon? Have faith in the gifts God has placed in your life. Ask for God's help, and run the race God has placed before you.

Just say grace.
—GOD

By grace are ye saved through faith; and
that not of yourselves: it is the gift of God.

Ephesians 2:8 KJV

Do you ever feel inadequate? Unworthy? Most of us do from time to time. And we all know people we think are too successful to have those same feelings.

Martin Luther, the sixteenth-century German preacher and Bible scholar who initiated the Protestant Reformation, sounds like the type of man who would be eminently sure of himself. Any man who would dare to publicly question the theology of his church—in a time when it could cost him his life—could not be a man who had doubts about himself. Or could he be?

In truth, Luther spent his early years obsessed by his presumed unworthiness. But one day while reading the Bible, Luther realized that he could not earn his salvation. He read in the book of Romans that we *receive* God's love and mercy. We don't *earn* it. It is a gift—a priceless gift that cost the life of God's own Son.

On days when you fall flat on your face or just feel low, remind yourself that your mistakes aren't the end of the world. Your relationship with God doesn't depend on how well you manage to color inside the lines. God loves you, and He realizes that you aren't perfect. Receive His grace today.

You're always welcome.
—GOD

Commit to the LORD whatever you do,
and your plans will succeed.

Proverbs 16:3

A poor young artist called her aunt one day to let her know that she was leaving on a trip to try to sell her wood carvings of sea birds to the owner of the gift shop at a fashionable resort. She asked her aunt to pray that her venture would be successful. Her aunt assured her that she would pray for the largest order she had ever received!

That evening, the young artist called her aunt back. With great exuberance she told her aunt what had happened. Not only had the gift-shop owner purchased all of her carvings, but the owner of a chain of gift shops had ordered as many carvings as she could make! She was filled with wonder at how abundantly God had answered prayer. "Now," she said to her aunt, "pray that I can fill his order!"

Her aunt wisely replied, "The Lord doesn't open a door for us unless He expects us to walk through it successfully. When you pray for rain, don't be surprised when you get a cloudburst!"

When you ask for God's help, are you expecting a bare-minimum, meager-but-satisfactory answer or no answer at all? God wants to help you succeed in all of your endeavors. Open your arms and receive His blessing. He is always glad to help![16]

I make happy endings.
—GOD

"Do not let your hearts be troubled.
Trust in God; trust also in me."

John 14:1

Robert and his wife were in shock when their dream cabin overlooking Mount Timpanogos was crushed in an avalanche. It took nature only ten seconds to destroy what had taken them several years to design, plan, build, and furnish. They had a very difficult time seeing God in the situation as they picked through the smashed bits of their belongings.

Eight months later, a colleague told Robert about an accident their wives had almost had on the day of the avalanche. The man's wife and son, coming down the narrow road from their cabin, had skidded on the icy pavement and almost collided with Robert's wife, who was on her way up the hill. Just before the two vehicles collided, the man's wife turned her car into a deep snow bank.

It took almost an hour to get the vehicle unstuck. While they worked, Robert's wife and son also waited, unable to pass. Had the accident not occurred, they would very likely have been at home, killed in the avalanche!

Be slow to judge devastating circumstances in your life. Trouble does not come from God, but He is ever present to turn those things around for your good. Ask Him to show you His hand of protection in every situation.[17]

Remember your sins? I forgot them. —GOD

I will forgive their wickedness and will remember their sins no more.

Hebrews 8:12

In 1969, millions of people watched the televised Apollo 11 takeoff that launched three men into space. Those three men would become the first humans to land on the moon.

One of the remarkable facts about this space trip was that more energy was used in the first few minutes during and after liftoff than during the next several days of traveling half-a-million miles to the moon. Tremendous energy was needed to break the spacecraft out of the earth's powerful gravitational pull and set it free to reach its destination.

The memory of past mistakes and failures can serve as the gravitational pull that slows us down and keeps us from going upward and onward in our lives. That's why it's so important to lay our past failures at God's feet. The Bible says that when we confess our sins to God, He forgives us and casts our shortcomings and sins into a sea of forgetfulness. That's right! He not only forgives, He also forgets.

If your past mistakes are dragging you down and keeping you from being all you can be, ask God to forgive you. Then thank Him as you feel yourself breaking free and soaring to new heights.

Read the Bible and prevent truth decay.
—GOD

The whole Bible was given to us by inspiration from God and is useful to teach us what is true and to make us realize what is wrong in our lives.

2 Timothy 3:16 TLB

Abraham Lincoln repeatedly referred to his indebtedness to and regard for the Bible. He began reading it as a boy and its influence over him increased as the years went by.

Whenever he addressed the public, Lincoln quoted from the Bible more than from any other book, and his literary style mirrored the style of the Bible, especially the writings of the prophets. His respect for the Bible is also apparent in the ideals he espoused and the principles by which he lived.

Lincoln felt keenly his responsibility to guide our great nation through a time of unprecedented turmoil. His response to that responsibility was anchored firmly in his belief that the Bible is God's Word, penned by the hands of the apostles and prophets. By reading and meditating on its principles, Lincoln believed he could keep himself and the nation squarely on the path of truth.

Take a long look at your life. Are you searching for truth? If so, take time to find a Bible. There are many newer translations that make it easier to read and understand. One of our nation's greatest presidents considered it a priceless weapon in the pursuit of truth. You will surely find the same.

Flee temptation—and don't leave a forwarding address.
—GOD

"Get up and pray so that you will not fall into temptation."

Luke 22:46

According to an old legend, two monks named Tanzan and Ekido were traveling together down a muddy road one day. Heavy monsoon rains had saturated the area, and they were grateful for a few moments of sunshine to make their journey. Before long, they came around a bend and encountered a lovely girl in a silk kimono. She looked forlorn as she stared at the muddy road before her.

At once, Tanzan responded to her plight. "Come here, girl," he said. Then lifting her in his arms, he carried her over the slippery ooze to the other side of the road.

Ekido didn't speak again to Tanzan. Then that night after they reached their intended lodging, Ekido could no longer restrain his anger and disappointment. "We monks don't go near women," he said to Tanzan in an accusing voice. "Why did you do that?"

"I left the girl back there, Ekido," replied Tanzan. "Are you still carrying her?"

Ekido thought that he had insulated himself from temptation by constructing rigid laws of conduct. Because he was focused on the letter of the law, he succumbed to the temptation to be ruled by anger, resentment, intolerance, and a lack of kindness. Don't be fooled; only God can help you master temptation by writing His living laws upon your heart.

Love one another. Is that so hard? —GOD

*Dear friends, let us love one another,
for love comes from God.*

1 John 4:7

Love is the most popular theme on earth. It dominates music, literature, art, motion pictures, and every other aspect of our culture. We all want to be loved. In fact, we all need to be loved. That is the way God made us.

Love, however, is both difficult to give and difficult to receive. Selfishness and pride often keep us from the greatest gift God has to offer. If you have found it hard to give and receive love, you may well have been looking in the wrong place. Real love comes from God. It is the very essence of His being. It is impossible to be in His presence without experiencing the power of love. It is impossible to experience His love without passing that love along.

Don't let pride and selfishness keep you from finding, receiving, and sharing the love you need to live a happy, fulfilled, and satisfying life. Look to the Source of all love, God Himself. He will fill you up until His love literally overflows onto those around you.

And don't worry, the Bible says God's love is limitless and unconditional. Once you lock into the Source, your search will be over and your life will never be the same.

Need a hug?
—GOD

God demonstrates his own love for us in this:
While we were still sinners, Christ died for us.

Romans 5:8

Babe Ruth hit 714 home runs during his baseball career, but on this particular day toward the end of his career, the Braves were playing the Reds in Cincinnati, and the great Bambino was no hero. He bumbled the ball and threw badly. In one inning alone, his errors were responsible for most of the five runs scored by Cincinnati.

As the Babe walked off the field and headed toward the dugout after the third out, a crescendo of angry cries and boos rose to greet him. Then a boy jumped over the railing and ran out onto the field. With tears streaming down his face, he threw his arms around the legs of his hero.

Ruth didn't hesitate for a second. He picked up the boy, hugged him, then set him down and patted his head. The cries from the crowd abruptly stopped. A hush fell over the entire park. In that brief moment, the fans saw two heroes on the field: Ruth who, in spite of his own dismal day in fielding, cared about the feelings of a young fan and a boy who cared about the feelings of another human being.

No matter what your performance has been on the playing field of life, God has a hug waiting for you. He is your number-one fan.

Smile–
I love you!
—GOD

I have loved you with an everlasting love;
I have drawn you with loving-kindness.

Jeremiah 31:3

Why God loves us is a mystery—one we will never solve. The good news is that we don't have to understand why; He just does! The Bible says that God's love is a gift—pure and simple. It's not something we have earned. We haven't charmed our way into God's heart. We haven't impressed Him with our selfless acts or great charitable contributions. God loves us because He chooses to.

So why do we struggle so hard to receive it and why do so many people pass through this life without ever feeling the warmth of God's loving smile? Perhaps it's because we are so busy working to make ourselves worthy of His love that we somehow miss the simple truth of it.

You will never be good enough, cute enough, bright enough, accomplished enough, or rich enough to earn God's love. Nor will you ever be able to understand it. But receiving it is easy. All you have to do is reach out and take it.

Open the door to your heart today. Look up into God's loving face and smile at this blessing. Then close your eyes and imagine Him smiling back at you. God loves you!

Planning for your future? I am.
—GOD

*No eye has seen, no ear has heard,
no mind has conceived what God has
prepared for those who love him.*

1 Corinthians 2:9

In *Beyond Ourselves*, author Catherine Marshall tells about a problem she faced as a young person. She and her family lived in a small town in West Virginia that had undergone severe financial struggles in the aftermath of the 1929 stock-market crash. The two railroad shops, which were the only industry in town, were nearly shut down. Even with the promise of a small work scholarship and the $125 she had saved, Catherine was several hundred dollars short of what she needed to attend college.

One night her mother came to her room and found her sobbing. Her dreams of college seemed dashed. Her mother suggested that they bow together and ask for God's help. "Whenever we ask God for something that is His will, He hears us," her mother said. "If He hears us, then He grants the request we have made. So you and I can rest on that promise."

Soon, Catherine's mother was offered a job writing the history of their county. She made enough in this job to pay for Catherine's college expenses with a little to spare.

Do you have plans and goals for your life that seem impossible to achieve? Ask God to help. He will open doors of opportunity for you that you never imagined. He is committed to your success.[18]

Want to talk?
—GOD

I will hear, for I am compassionate.

Exodus 22:27

Many people see God as a stern judge, just waiting to pounce on those who break His laws. Others see Him as the supreme power of the universe, distant and remote, uninvolved in their lives. But there are also those who enjoy a loving, open relationship with their heavenly Father.

How we perceive God has a direct impact on how we pray. If we see God as a stern judge, we may not be brave enough to speak to Him at all. If we see Him as distant and remote, we may dismiss Him from our lives completely. However, if we see God as our loving, generous, heavenly Father, we are likely to talk to Him about everything.

How do you see God? The Bible says that He is filled with compassion toward us and is ready to hear us when we call out to Him for help. Yes, one day He will be the great judge of all the earth. But you have been invited to know Him first as Father and friend.

God has made an eternal commitment to love and nurture you. At great personal cost, He has opened the lines of communication so that you can speak to Him without fear. He has promised to hear every word. What are you waiting for?

I still create rainbows.
—GOD

*We know that God is always at work
for the good of everyone who loves him.*

Romans 8:28 CEV

One Christmas Eve, a man was driving two young women to church when they came upon a multiple-car collision. They were unable to stop on the slick road and slammed into the back of a car. One of the girls, Donna, was thrown face-first through the windshield. The jagged edges of the broken windshield made two deep gashes in her left cheek.

At the hospital, the doctor on duty happened to be a plastic surgeon. He took great care in stitching Donna's face. Nevertheless, the driver was devastated by what had happened.

A short time later Donna's family moved away. Fifteen years passed before the driver happened to see Donna's mother, who gave him the following report. "Donna was so intrigued by her hospital stay that she became a nurse, got a good job at a hospital, met a young doctor, married him, and then had two children. God took a stormy day and created a beautiful rainbow. Donna told me that the accident was the best thing that could have happened to her!"

God is not the initiator of tragedy and suffering in our lives, but He is always there to bring some good to every situation. If you are in the midst of a fierce storm, don't lose hope. Look for the rainbow![19]

Wanna play "Follow the Leader"?
—GOD

"I have set you an example that you should do as I have done."

John 13:15

The story is told of a Christian missionary who was lost at sea and by chance, washed up on an island near a remote native village. Finding him half dead from starvation and exposure, the people of the village nursed him back to health. He subsequently lived among the people for some twenty years. Since he could not speak their language, he could not confess his faith or preach any sermons to them.

However, when the people were sick, he attended them. When they were hungry, he gave them food. When they were lonely, he kept them company. He taught the ignorant and came to the aid of those who were wronged.

One day missionaries came to the village and began talking to the people about a man called Jesus. After hearing what they had to say of Jesus' ministry and teachings, they insisted that He had been living among them for twenty years.

If you have experienced the miracle of God's love and grace, you may be anxious to share that with others. Just remember that your words will never be as important as your actions. Those around you will know that what you have found is real by witnessing the difference it makes in your life.[20]

Pssst . . .
up here!
—GOD

Never will I leave you; never will I forsake you.

Hebrews 13:5

A church once sent a man to spend two months as a volunteer at Mother Teresa's mission in Calcutta, caring for India's sick, poor, and dying. He left on his mission with great joy—a dream come true.

Standing by a luggage carousel in Bangkok, forty hours later, he felt anything but elation. Somewhere between South Korea and Thailand, his luggage had been "misdirected." His nerves worn raw by sleeplessness, he collapsed into a nearby chair and wondered, *Was this trip a mistake?* He felt as lost as his bags.

As his eyes wandered around the walls of the lobby, which was mostly empty owing to the late hour, he noticed a row of clocks on one wall. They displayed the time in London, New York, Sydney, and Bangkok. He quickly noted that it was noon at his home church—and it was Sunday.

His church had promised to pray for him at noon services that day. *They're praying for me right now,* he thought. And with that realization came a tremendous peace. *I'm not alone now. And I won't be alone in the months ahead!*

God knows your needs, and no matter where you are, He is with you, hearing your prayers and working on your behalf. When your circumstances start to bring you down—look up![21]

You're always on My mind.
—GOD

Let him who walks in the dark, who has no light,
trust in the name of the LORD and rely on his God.

Isaiah 50:10

Almost every kid has experienced the excitement and intrigue of a backyard camp out. Dad helping to put up the tent and Mom pulling together enough snacks to get the eager beavers through the night. Then armed with flashlights, pocketknives, and the faithful family dog, the campers faced the elements.

If you've been on one of these daring adventures, you know the one thing no one counts on is the darkness. The trees in the yard, so innocent by day, cast menacing shadows at night. Unfamiliar sounds, impossible to identify in the dark, begin to wear away at your resolve. The whole thing starts to feel pretty scary. Just when you're about to bolt for the house, you look up and see Mom and Dad watching from the window, ready to rescue you at a moment's notice.

The world can be a dark, scary place. It can cast long, menacing shadows over our lives that leave us feeling alone and fearful. That's when we need to look up and see our heavenly Father watching, ready to chase away our fears and give us courage to make it through the night.

If your life is shrouded in darkness, know that God is with you. He will be there through the long night to comfort and strengthen you.

My line is never busy.
—GOD

The Lord is watching his children, listening to their prayers.

1 Peter 3:12 TLB

Three ministers were talking about prayer one day, and they began debating among themselves the most effective positions for prayer. As they talked, they were totally oblivious to a telephone repairman working on the phone system in a corner of the room where they were sitting.

One minister contended that the key to prayer was in the hands. He always held his hands together to show a firmness of commitment and then pointed his hands upward as a symbolic form of worship. The second minister countered that real prayer could only be made if a person was on his knees. To him, that was the proper position for submission to God. The third suggested that the best position was to pray while stretched out flat on one's face—the posture of supreme surrender.

By this time, the telephone repairman could no longer refrain from adding his opinion: "Well, I have found that the most powerful prayer I ever made was while I was suspended forty feet above the ground, dangling upside down by my heels from a telephone pole."

God doesn't care about the religious words connected with our prayers. He is always listening when we reach out to Him for help or just to talk. He can even hear your heart. Forget the formalities and give Him a call.[22]

Let's do life.
—GOD

I have come that they may have life, and that they may have it more abundantly.

John 10:10 NKJV

James Hewett wrote, "When I recognized this Higher Power, it seemed as though life was rather like a bike ride, but it was a tandem bike. God was in the back helping me pedal. I don't know just when it was that He suggested we change places, but life has not been the same since. When He took the lead, it was all I could do to hang on! He took me down delightful paths, up mountains and through rocky places—at breakneck speeds.

"I worried and was anxious and asked, 'Where are You taking me?' He laughed and didn't answer, and I started to learn trust. I forgot my boring life and entered into adventure. When I'd say, 'I'm scared,' He'd lean back and touch my hand.

"At first I did not trust Him to be in control of my life. I thought He'd wreck it, but He knows bike secrets—how to make it lean to take sharp corners, dodge large rocks, and speed through scary passages. I'm beginning to enjoy the view and the cool breeze on my face with my delightful, constant Companion."

Letting God have the front seat in your life can thrust you into an adventure you never imagined possible! The Master of the universe knows where all the good stuff is.[23]

It's getting dark—time to come home. —GOD

"Keep watch, because you do not know on what day your Lord will come."

Matthew 24:42

An old legend recounts how Satan once called three of his top aides to a special meeting so that they might make a plan about how to stop the effectiveness of a particular group of people. One of the aides, Resentment, proposed, "We should convince them there is no God." Satan sneered at Resentment and replied, "That would never work. They know there's a God."

Bitterness then spoke up: "We'll convince them that God does not really care about right or wrong." Satan thought about the idea for a few moments but then rejected it. "Too many know that God does care," he finally said.

Malice then proposed his idea. "We'll let them go on thinking there is a God and that He cares about right and wrong. But we will keep whispering that there is no hurry, there is no hurry, there is no hurry."

Satan howled with delight! The plan was adopted, and Malice was promoted to an even higher position in Satan's malevolent hierarchy.

If you have never given your heart to God, NOW is the time to reach out to Him. Don't be deceived. Today is the day of decision; tomorrow may be too late.

What are you doing for the rest of your life? —GOD

I have fought the good fight, I have finished the race, I have kept the faith.

2 Timothy 4:7

During the reign of Oliver Cromwell, the British government ran low on the silver they used to make their coins. Lord Cromwell sent his men to a local cathedral in search of silver. They reported, "The only silver we could find is in the statues of the saints standing in the corners." "Good!" Cromwell replied, "We'll melt down the saints and put them into circulation."

Circulating melted-down saints? It's an unusual metaphor but good theology! God never intended for us to be silver-plated, highly polished ornaments, solely for liturgical use. He intends for us to be living, breathing people, working together to accomplish His purposes in our lives.

God doesn't care about our money; He has all He needs. He doesn't care about our religious words or actions. He is more interested in the genuine good that flows from our hearts. He doesn't care about our social prowess; He is interested in our willingness to come humbly before Him with our prayers and petitions.

Has your relationship with God been just for show? If so, it's time to shed the unnecessary trappings that have kept you standing in the corner accomplishing nothing. God is waiting, always ready to help you become all that He intended for you to be.[24]

I made you, and I don't make mistakes.
—GOD

Remember your Creator in the days of your youth.

Ecclesiastes 12:1

As a boy, Steven was ambivalent about his Jewish heritage. To him, being Jewish often meant not being part of the "normal" world. Christmastime was especially tough since he lived on a block that won awards for its Christmas decorations, with the exception of his home, which he dubbed "the black hole."

His sense of being different was heightened when his family moved to a Phoenix neighborhood with very few Jews. Then, when his father took a job in northern California, he experienced overt anti-Semitism for the first time. Some of his high-school peers openly ridiculed him, and one bully routinely hit him during flag football games.

Years later, when his son, Max, was born, Steven Spielberg came to grips with his Jewish heritage. Although he believed other filmmakers were better suited for the project, he proudly embraced the responsibility to make the film, *Schindler's List*. In accepting and appreciating who he was, Spielberg fulfilled himself both artistically and personally.

God has created each one of us with unique gifts and talents that can be expressed by no one else. Express your real self today—without compromise. God has a wonderful plan for your life, and no one can fulfill that plan but YOU![25]

OK, break it up!
—GOD

"A new command I give you:
Love one another."

John 13:34

One day, three rough-looking fellows on huge motor-cycles pulled up to a highway café. Inside, they found only a waitress, the cook, and one truck driver—a little guy perched on a stool at the counter, quietly eating his lunch.

The motorcyclists, angry that a trucker had cut them off several miles back, decided to hassle this innocent man. They grabbed his food and mocked him, laughing in his face and calling him bad names. The truck driver said nothing. He simply got up, paid for his food, and walked out.

One of the three men, unhappy that they hadn't succeeded in provoking the little man into a fist fight, said to the waitress, "He sure wasn't much of a man, was he?"

The waitress replied, "I guess not." Then looking out the window, she added, "I guess he's not much of a truck driver either. He just ran over three motorcycles on his way out of the parking lot."

Many of the problems we face in life are of our own making. If you find that your life keeps hitting snags because of inappropriate behaviors or improper choices, it's time to make a change. God won't condemn you for the past. But He will give you the courage to make your future a better place to live.

Courage is fear that has said its prayers.
—GOD

Keep alert. Be firm in your faith.
Stay brave and strong.

1 Corinthians 16:13 CEV

At age thirty-three, golfer Paul Azinger was at the top of his game. He had only one problem: a nagging pain in his right shoulder, which had been operated on in 1991. After seeing the doctor, Paul received a call that changed his life. His doctor wanted him back in Los Angeles immediately for a biopsy.

Paul forged a compromise: He'd do it as soon as he had played in the PGA Championship tournament and the Ryder Cup Challenge. Until then, he would rely on medication and prayer. He tried to convince himself he had tendinitis, but the pain grew worse. Ultimately, he learned he had cancer.

One morning while praying in his bedroom, Paul was wondering what would happen if he didn't get better. Suddenly the sun seemed to force its way through the blinds and a powerful feeling of peace swelled within him. He knew with absolute assurance that God was with him.

Two years later, Paul rejoined the pro tour—the cancer gone. He says that his main goal in life now has shifted from winning to helping people see that "God is there for them."

Are you looking for the courage to face a difficult situation in your life? Don't let fear push you around. Place yourself in God's hands.

I love to hear you laugh. —GOD

The joy of the LORD is your strength.

Nehemiah 8:10

Jay Kesler once wrote in *Campus Life* magazine, "There are two ways of handling pressure. One is illustrated by a bathysphere, the miniature submarine used to explore the ocean in places so deep that the water pressure would crush a conventional submarine like an aluminum can. Bathyspheres compensate with plate steel several inches thick, which keeps the water out but also makes them heavy and hard to maneuver. Inside they're cramped.

"When these craft descend to the ocean floor, however, they find they're not alone. When their lights are turned on and you look through the tiny, thick plate-glass windows, what do you see? Fish!

"These fish cope with the extreme pressure in an entirely different way. They don't build thick skins: They remain supple and free. They compensate for the outside pressure through equal and opposite pressure inside themselves."

What a marvelous analogy for the gift of laughter God has given us. It helps us "equalize" the pressures that come to bear on us in life. It helps us avoid exploding or imploding. While we should never laugh at the expense of others, it is a wonderful idea to laugh at life a little every day. Or, if you like, laugh a lot![26]

If you listen to me whisper now, I won't have to shout later.
—GOD

Listen and hear my voice;
pay attention and hear what I say.

Isaiah 28:23

One day, an old woman went to Anthony Bloom and told him that while she had constantly recited the prayer of Jesus for many years, she had never really experienced the presence of God.

Bloom replied, "How can God get a word in edgeways if you never stop talking? Give him a chance. Keep quiet."

"How can I do that?" she asked. He then gave her this advice, which he later gave to many others. He advised her to tidy her room each day after breakfast, making it as pleasant as possible. Then, to sit down in a position where she could see the entire room, including the window that looked out on the garden.

"When you have sat down, rest for a quarter of an hour in the presence of God, but take care not to pray," Bloom said. "Be as quiet as you can and as you obviously can't do *nothing*, knit before the Lord and tell me what happens." She returned several days later, happy to report that at long last she had felt the presence of God!

God most often speaks to us in a still, small voice; therefore, it takes a still, quiet heart to hear Him. Practice being quiet before Him and see what happens. He may have something important to tell you.[27]

FYI: My last name isn't "Dang-it." —GOD

Stop all your dirty talk. Say the right thing at the right time and help others by what you say.

Ephesians 4:29 CEV

A man once sat down to have dinner with his family. As was their tradition, the family members joined hands around the table, and the man said a rote prayer, thanking God for the food, the hands that had prepared it, and for the source of all life. During the meal, however, he bitterly cursed his job and his boss and complained at length about the staleness of the bread and a bit of mold he found on one edge of the brick of cheese.

One night his young daughter asked him, "Daddy, do you think God heard you say grace before the meal?"

"Of course, honey," he answered confidently.

Then she asked, "Do you think God heard everything you said during dinner?" The man answered, "Why, yes, I believe so. God hears everything."

She thought for a moment and then asked, "Daddy, which one do you think God believed—what you said before we ate or what you said while we were eating?"

God hears everything we say—the good and the bad—and so do the people around us. Honor God in all that you say, and His blessing will rest on your life as well as the lives of those who hear and heed your example.

I'm just a prayer away.
—GOD

Be joyful in hope, patient in affliction, faithful in prayer.

Romans 12:12

A man who owned a plot of land was about to leave the area on a journey that would take several years. Before he left, he leased his land to others. When he returned, he discovered his renters had been very careless and brambles had sprung up, turning his plot of land into a wilderness of thorns. Desiring to cultivate the land, he sent his son to clear the ground.

The son quickly concluded, *It will take forever to get this land cleared!* Overwhelmed by the idea, he lay on the ground and went to sleep. He did the same day after day. Finally his father came to see what had been done and found the land untouched.

The son apologized to his father, explaining that the job had seemed so overwhelming that he had been afraid to tackle it. His father replied, "Son, if you had only cleared the area on which you lay down for a nap each day, your work would now be done."

You may be so overwhelmed by the challenges in your life that you wonder what good it would do to pray. But prayer by prayer, God can bring comfort and healing to your heart. Don't give up! God's mighty hand is only a prayer away.[28]

Don't make me come down there.
—GOD

"If you do not wake up, I will come like a thief, and you will not know at what time I will come to you."

Revelation: 3:3

Many people act as if God is sitting up in Heaven taking care of the universe, not knowing or caring what we're up to down here on earth. But He does know! The Bible says that He knows every time a little sparrow falls to the ground.

God is watching. He sees us as we go through our daily lives—hearing what we say and noting what we do. He knows our deepest thoughts and most embarrassing secrets. He knows and loves us anyway.

God is loving, kind, and patient, but the Bible says He will not wait forever for us to get our ducks in a row. One day, He will come back and hold us accountable for how we have lived our lives. The Bible says that we will not know when that day of reckoning will occur. Therefore, we are to live our lives in a prudent manner.

How are you living your life? Will you be embarrassed to face your Creator when He arrives? If so, make your peace with Him now. Open your heart and ask Him to clean you up and make you ready for the day He will come down here.

They're commandments, not suggestions. —GOD

"If you love me, you will obey what I command."

John 14:15

Thirty years ago, Sandy Koufax, a Jewish pitcher for the Los Angeles Dodgers, announced that he wouldn't play on the holiest day of his year, Yom Kippur. Koufax's employer pointed out that it was the first game of the 1965 World Series. Couldn't he pitch just a little? "No," Koufax said. But, he pitched a shutout in games five and seven, and the Dodgers won the series 4-3.

In 1996, Eli Herring, a 340-pound offensive tackle, who sported a 3.5 grade-point average, was expected to be the top senior offensive tackle in the pro draft. However, he turned down a possible multimillion-dollar deal with the Oakland Raiders because he wouldn't play on his holy day, Sunday.

Do you think these men made foolish decisions? They would be likely to tell you that the opposite is true. God's commandments are designed to keep us on the path to happiness and well-being. They are designed to remind us of basic truths, such as the fact that fame and fortune are fleeting, but keeping our word and honoring our convictions add character to our lives—character that will serve us well in the storms of life.

Do you have solid convictions to guide you? It may be time to establish or reaffirm a strong foundation for your life.[29]

Alone you can't.
Together we can.
—GOD

"With God all things are possible."

Matthew 19:26

While skiing in Colorado one day, a man noticed some people on the slope wearing red vests. Moving closer, he could read these words on their vests: BLIND SKIER. The statement intrigued him. He had difficulty skiing with 20/20 vision! How could people without sight manage?

Soon he discovered their secret. Each skier had a guide who skied beside, behind, or in front of him but always in a place where the two could easily communicate. The guide used two basic forms of communication. First, tapping the ski poles together to assure the blind person that he was there and second, speaking simple, specific directions: "Go right. Turn left. Slow. Stop. Skier on your right."

We can't see even five seconds into the future. We cannot see the struggles to come or other people who may run into us or we into them, like errant skiers on a crowded slope. But God has promised to be our guide through life—to walk before and behind us and to dwell in us. It is our role to listen and to obey.

You may be facing a slippery slope today and the prospect of making it to the bottom without any idea what challenges you will face along the way. Let God be your guide. Together you can make it![30]

Whatever your lot in life, build something on it.
—GOD

Whatever your hand finds to do,
do it with all your might.

Ecclesiastes 9:10

Richard Foster wrote: "I had come to Kotzebue on the adventure of helping to 'build the first high school above the Arctic Circle,' but the work itself was far from an adventure. It was hard, backbreaking labor.

"One day I was trying to dig a trench for a sewer line— no small task in a world of frozen tundra. An Eskimo man, whose face and hands displayed the leathery toughness of many winters, came by and watched me for a while. Finally he said simply and profoundly, 'You are digging a ditch to the glory of God.'

"He said it to encourage me, I know. And I have never forgotten his words. Beyond my Eskimo friend, no human being ever knew or cared whether I dug that ditch well or poorly. In time it was to be covered up and forgotten. But because of my friend's words, I dug with all my might, for every shovelful of dirt was a prayer to God."

God has given each of us certain gifts and talents. He knows that using those gifts and talents to the fullest is the very thing that will bring us satisfaction and fulfillment. Are you using the gifts God has entrusted to you to the fullest? That is the road to true happiness.[31]

I'm listening.
—GOD

The righteous cry out, and the LORD hears them;
he delivers them from all their troubles.

Psalm 34:17

Today we live in an environment of high anxiety. More people than ever before are seeking professional help to deal with the stress and depression caused by our modern lifestyles.

Many individuals require antidepressant drugs that counter the effects of chemical imbalances, but the most physically balanced person on the planet will still feel the challenge of dealing with complications and questions that were unheard of just fifty years ago.

The Bible says that God is our high tower, a refuge in time of trouble. When we feel anxious and overwhelmed, God has promised to fill us with His peace that passes understanding, sheltering us from the torment of our worry and restoring us once again to soundness. He has promised never to leave us, to be always available to help us when we cry out to Him.

Where do you turn when the extremities of life seem to have you cornered? Do you reach out to God? He understands what you are facing today. He knows the boundaries of your strength and courage. He wants to reach out to you with His peace. Call on Him and you will feel His calm assurance that together you can handle whatever life dishes out.

Got me?
—GOD

I will put my Spirit in you and you will live.

Ezekiel 37:14

There are moments in each of our lives when we seem to be drowning in the turbulent emotions of a desperate crisis. At those times, it may seem difficult to reach out to God and receive His comfort. But those are also the times when we need Him most.

It grieves God to see us try to endure those troubling times alone, to hear our agony as if we were on the other side of a closed door. He could come crashing through the door, but that is not His way. He has placed within each of us a free will, a freedom of choice that He will not override.

No matter what you may be going through today, your best recourse is to invite God to come inside and touch your hurting heart with His loving, healing hand. You may be too confused and distraught to know what you need. But He knows. And once you invite Him in, He will give you all the strength, encouragement, love, and comfort you need.

Don't face the tragedies of your life alone. Reach out and unlock the door. No matter what you are facing, He is the answer.

I was—I am—
I always will be.
—GOD

I the LORD do not change.

Malachi 3:6

One of the most magnificent truths about God is that He meets us in every moment of prayer with the fullness of His being. He reveals Himself to us as I AM, ever present and available. He brings the fullness of who He is to each moment of our lives. He brings not just a part of Himself but all of Himself—His majesty, power, wisdom, and love.

Our best and highest response to such marvelous access to the fullness of the holy, omnipotent, infinite King of the universe must surely be one of awe. It matters very little what we say. Just to be in His presence and to simultaneously be aware of His presence is to be put into a position of humility, need, and provision.

Rousseau once noted, "To write a good love letter, you will begin without knowing what you are going to say and end without knowing what you have said." The same is true of prayer. Being in God's presence and having a relationship with Him is all that matters.

God wants to reveal Himself to you. Close your eyes and open your heart. Pour out your soul freely. Don't think about what you are going to say. Just relax and renew yourself in His presence. He's waiting for you right now.

Need directions?
—GOD

*Trust in the LORD with all your heart
and lean not on your own understanding;
in all your ways acknowledge him, and
he will make your paths straight.*

Proverbs 3:5-6

No matter who you are and what you do, it's a sure thing you won't be living on this earth forever. So, when your time here on earth comes to an end, where will you be? What will you have? What will you do?

Whether we like it or not, we are all traveling—somewhere. From the day we are born, we are really capable of going in only two directions: Either we are headed toward God or away from Him. Despite what we would sometimes like to think, there is no middle ground. All our thoughts, choices, and actions really add up to one very important decision: Which way will we go?

The Almighty God of all wants you. He wants to put you on the path that leads to Him. He wants you to be in His presence for eternity. There are no guarantees about tomorrow. So, don't wait any longer to call on Him. This moment is the only one that matters.

Which road are you headed down? Is it the right one? Will it take you to your heavenly Father? If you ask Him, He will be happy—yes, most delighted—to direct you to His place!

You think it's hot here? —GOD

God did not send his Son into the world to condemn the world, but to save the world through him.

John 3:17

It's fun to speculate about Heaven. What will we do? What will a life without pain and fear be like? Will Heaven's streets *really* be gold or is that just a biblical metaphor?

But what about life in the *other* place? That's not a pleasant topic. Theologians speculate and debate what hell will be like (e.g., "Is it a real location—or just a metaphysical state?" "Is it really hot there—or is *that* just a metaphor?").

Like Heaven, hell is a mystery to us. But two things are certain. First, hell is something separated from God's love, from His grace. Second, hell's gates are shut from the *inside*. The Bible makes it clear that God calls out to us, urging us to come to Him. God's Word assures us that He doesn't want anyone to perish.

So, the next time you're on your way to an earthly destination—work, home, the movies—take some time to consider your ultimate destination. Do you want to spend the afterlife basking in God's love and mercy? Or filled with the regret and anguish that come from rejecting His love and mercy? Eternity is a long time to spend separated from the One who loves you more than anyone in the universe. Choose wisely. Your choice makes a world of difference.

I'm the only one who really knows what time it is.
—GOD

"No one knows about that day or hour, not even the angels in heaven, nor the Son, but only the Father."

Mark 13:32

The Bible says that God has set into motion an eternal plan—a plan that includes a new Heaven and a new earth. A world devoid of suffering and pain, hate and murder, corruption and death. It is described as a world where the ravages of pollution and decay have been erased and the earth has been returned to the glory of its original creation.

On that earth, God will dwell in sweet communion with those who have chosen to make Him part of their lives. The tears of sorrow shed for those who have turned their backs on His love will by then be in the past. Instead, tears of joy will flow down His face onto those who have chosen to receive the riches of His compassion, mercy, and loving-kindness.

Only God knows how long it will be before the next step in His divine plan begins to play itself out. The Bible tells us that we cannot even imagine all that God has in store for those who have claimed their place in His kingdom.

Don't miss your opportunity to be part of God's eternal plan. Don't let His invitation to live forever in the light of His presence lie on your desk unopened until it's too late. Say yes. Give Him your heart!

Believe me now.
See me later.
—GOD

*"My sheep recognize my voice, and I know
them, and they follow me. I give them
eternal life and they shall never perish.
No one shall snatch them away from me."*

John 10:27-28 TLB

God is patient, loving, and kind. He has plans for you—plans for a future grander than anything you could imagine—but time is running out. In the Bible, He says that His desire is for every person to be part of His plans. But He knows that many will perish in the stormy waters of willfulness and pride, stubbornly refusing His offer to take His hand and be brought safely into the boat.

The Bible says that one day everyone will believe, because they will experience the consequences of their decision to turn their backs on God. But by then, some fates will be sealed—the result of their choice, not God's. Eternity without God is unthinkable—eternal separation from Him, tormented by the wrong choice. If only they had listened. If only. . . .

There's an old saying: Hell is paved with good intentions. Someday, they intended to follow God. Someday, they were going to make Him their top priority. Someday, they were going to learn more about His plans. But someday never came. Death intervened.

God is calling to you. His words of invitation have been delivered to your heart. Are you going to respond? Believe Him now. He loves you and wants you to follow Him!

GodSpeaks Topical Index

Comfort and Encouragement

The Power of Prayer

God's Nature

Words of Wisdom

God's Eternal Love

The Ultimate Choice

References

Endnotes

1   *You Can Make a Difference*, Earl Babbie (NY: St. Martin's Press, 1985), p. 506.

2   *Encyclopedia of 7700 Illustrations*, Paul Lee Tan, ed. (Rockville, MD: Assurance Publishers, 1979), # 1230.

3   *Guideposts*, July 1995, p. 5.

4   *Mourning Into Dancing*, Walter Wangerin Jr. (Grand Rapids, MI: Zondervan, 1992), pp. 266-268.

5   *Encyclopedia of 7700 Illustrations*, Paul Lee Tan, ed. (Rockville, MD: Assurance Publishers, 1979), #4573.

6   *Sin, Sex, and Self-Control*, Norman Vincent Peale (NY: Doubleday and Co., 1965), pp. 160-161.

7   *My Utmost for His Highest*, Oswald Chambers (Grand Rapids, MI: Discovery House Publishers, 1992).

8   *Encyclopedia of 7700 Illustrations*, Paul Lee Tan, ed. (Rockville, MD: Assurance Publishers, 1979), pp. 2058-2059.

9   *Encyclopedia of 7700 Illustrations*, Paul Lee Tan, ed. (Rockville, MD: Assurance Publishers, 1979), #4638.

10 *Encyclopedia of Sermon Illustrations*, David F. Burgess, ed. (St. Louis, MO: Concordia Publishing House, 1984), p. 159.

11 *Encyclopedia of 7700 Illustrations*, Paul Lee Tan, ed. (Rockville, MD: Assurance Publishers, 1979), p. 1257.

12 *Reader's Digest*, May 1996, pp. 169-172.

13 *Illustrations Unlimited*, James S. Hewett (Wheaton, IL: Tyndale, 1988), pp. 55-56.

14 *Inspirational Study Bible*, Max Lucado, ed. (Dallas, TX: Word, 1995), pp. 330, 331.

15 *Life's Bottom Line*, Richard Exley (Tulsa, OK: Honor Books, 1990), p. 28.

16 *The Guideposts Handbook of Prayer*, Phyllis Hobe (Carmel, NY: Guideposts, 1982), p. 72.

17 *A 3rd Serving of Chicken Soup for the Soul*, Jack Canfield and Mark Victor Hansen (Deerfield Beach, FL: Health Communications, 1996), pp. 211-214.

18 *Beyond Ourselves*, Catherine Marshall, (Carmel, NY: Guideposts, 1961), pp. 72-74.

19 *A 3rd Serving of Chicken Soup for the Soul*, Jack Canfield and Mark Victor Hansen (Deerfield Beach, FL: Health Communications, 1996), pp. 220-222.

20 *Illustrations Unlimited*, James S. Hewett (Wheaton, IL: Tyndale, 1988), pp. 361-362.

21 *Guideposts*, July 1995, p. 12.

22 *Illustrations Unlimited*, James Hewett, ed. (Wheaton, IL: Tyndale House, 1988), pp. 418-419.

23 *Illustrations Unlimited*, James S. Hewett (Wheaton, IL: Tyndale, 1988), pp. 247-248.

24 *On the Anvil*, Max Lucado, (Wheaton, IL: Tyndale House, 1985) pp. 21-22.

25 *Reader's Digest*, April 1996, pp. 71-76.

26 Anecdote from James S. Hewett, *Illustrations Unlimited*, (Wheaton, IL: Tyndale, 1988), p. 486.

27 *The Guideposts Handbook of Prayer*, Phyllis Hobe (Carmel, NY: Guideposts, 1982), p. 47.

28 *To Pray and to Love*, Robert Bondi (Minneapolis, MN: Fortress Press, 1991), p. 57.

29 *Reader's Digest*, April 1996, p. 185.

30 *Hearing God*, Peter Lord (Grand Rapids, MI: Baker Book House, 1988), p. 18.

31 *Seeking the Kingdom*, Richard J. Foster (San Francisco, CA: HarperSan Francisco, 1995), p. 101.

Additional copies of this book and other
titles in the *GodSpeaks*™ series
are available from your local bookstore.

If you have enjoyed this book, or if it has impacted your life,
we would like to hear from you.

Please contact us at:

Honor Books
Department E
P.O. Box 55388
Tulsa, Oklahoma 74155

Or by e-mail at *info@honorbooks.com*

Honor Books
Tulsa, Oklahoma

Dear One,

If this book has been a thought-provoking journey for you and you would like to learn more about Me, spend some time reading My Bible. Find one that speaks to you in your everyday language.

Most of all, I want to develop a relationship with you. Talk to Me, and listen to what I have to say. Join a Bible study group and find a church where you can fellowship with other people who love Me. Ask lots of questions. Tell them you're new at this "God thing." They'll understand.

And remember . . . you are never alone. I am always with you.

Love,
GOD

We invite you to learn more about the GodSpeaks™
campaign by contacting us at our website:

www.GodSpeaks.org